The Best Places to Visit on the Amalfi Coast Before You Kick The Bucket

The ultimate pocket travel guide with the best restaurants and must-see beaches

Kevin Johnson

Contents

Introduction

Welcome to the Amalfi Coast, a beautiful and historical region located in southern Italy known for its stunning landscape, delicious Italian cuisine, and excellent wines. Nestled along the Mediterranean Sea, the Amalfi Coast is home to several small villages and towns, each with its unique character and history.

One of the main attractions of the Amalfi Coast is its beautiful beaches, including the beach at Positano, often called one of the most beautiful beaches in the world. In addition to its beautiful beaches, the Amalfi Coast is also known for its beautiful sunsets and clear waters, which make it a popular destination for swimming, snorkeling, and other water sports.

The Amalfi Coast is famous for tourists, and there are many different ways to travel around the region. The region is served by several bus routes, which can be a convenient and economical way to get around. If you are comfortable driving on winding and narrow roads, consider renting a car to explore the region at your own pace. Alternatively, you can travel between the towns and villages by boat, which can be a fun and scenic way to see the coast. If you want a more organized and guided experience, consider booking a private tour of the region.

The Amalfi Coast is home to many excellent restaurants specializing in seafood dishes and excellent wines. The region is also home to several luxurious hotels, offering visitors a range of options for dining and accommodation.

Overall, the Amalfi Coast is a beautiful and vibrant region that offers something for everyone. Whether you are looking for beautiful beaches, delicious Italian cuisine, or a taste of history and culture, you will find it on the Amalfi Coast.

The History of The Amalfi coast

The Amalfi Coast is a stretch of coastline located on the southern coast of the Salerno Gulf in the Province of Salerno in southern Italy. It is located in the Campania region of Italy and is a popular tourist destination known for its rugged terrain, beautiful beaches, and charming towns.

The history of the Amalfi Coast dates back to ancient times. The ancient Greeks settled in the area and were later conquered by the Romans, who built several villas and mansions along the coast. In the Middle Ages, the region became an important maritime republic, with the town of Amalfi serving as a major trading center and naval power.

During this time, the Amalfi Coast became a thriving center of art, culture, and commerce. Many towns along the coast, such as Positano and Ravello, became wealthy and influential. The region also played a significant role in developing the Italian language and culture, with the Amalfi Coast serving as a melting pot of cultures and influences from around the Mediterranean.

The Amalfi Coast has become a popular tourist destination in the modern era, known for its stunning natural beauty and charming towns. Its picturesque villages, rugged coastline, and beautiful beaches attract visitors worldwide. The region is also home to many important cultural and historical sites, including the ruins of ancient Roman villas and the Amalfi Cathedral, a UNESCO World Heritage Site.

The Amalfi Coast is best known for its gorgeous and varied landscape, which includes rugged cliffs, secluded coves, and sandy beaches. The region is home to many charming towns and villages, each with its unique character and history.

One of the most famous towns on the Amalfi Coast is Amalfi, the largest town in the region and the namesake of the coast. Amalfi was once an important maritime republic and a major trading center in the Mediterranean. Today, it is known for its beautiful beaches, historic buildings, and charming narrow streets.

Other popular towns on the Amalfi Coast include Positano, Ravello, and Sorrento. Positano is a picturesque town known for its colorful houses, winding streets, and beautiful beaches. Ravello is a hilltop town that offers stunning views of the coast and is known for its beautiful gardens and villas. Sorrento is a popular tourist destination located on the Bay of Naples and is known for its beautiful beaches, charming streets, and excellent seafood.

In addition to its natural beauty and charming towns, the Amalfi Coast is also home to several important cultural and historical sites. The region is home to many ancient Roman villas, churches, and the Amalfi Cathedral, a UNESCO World Heritage Site. The Amalfi Coast is also known for its vibrant arts and crafts scene, with several local artisans producing handmade ceramics, jewelry, and other crafts.

Overall, the Amalfi Coast is a gorgeous and diverse region with a rich history and culture. Its stunning natural beauty, charming towns, and important cultural sites make it a must-visit destination for anyone interested in Italian history and culture.

What to Expect When on The Coast

Tourists visiting the Amalfi Coast can expect to experience a unique blend of natural beauty, charming towns, and rich cultural and historical sites. The region is known for its stunning coastline, rugged cliffs, secluded coves, sandy beaches, and charming towns and villages, each with its own character and history.

Tourists visiting the Amalfi Coast can expect to spend time exploring the region's beautiful natural surroundings, including its beaches, cliffs, and coves. Many visitors also enjoy hiking or walking along the coast to enjoy the stunning views.

In addition to its natural beauty, the Amalfi Coast is also known for its charming towns and villages, each with its own character and history. Visitors can expect to spend time exploring the narrow streets and charming squares of towns like Amalfi, Positano, and Sorrento and experiencing the local culture and traditions.

Tourists visiting the Amalfi Coast can also expect to have the opportunity to see many important cultural and historical sites, including ancient Roman villas and churches, as well as the Amalfi Cathedral, a UNESCO World Heritage Site. The region is also known for its vibrant arts and crafts scene, with several local artisans producing handmade ceramics, jewelry, and other crafts.

There are many other activities and attractions that tourists visiting the Amalfi Coast can enjoy. The region is known for its excellent food and wine, with several local restaurants and wineries offering delicious local specialties and internationally-renowned wines. Many visitors to the Amalfi Coast also enjoy participating in water sports, such as snorkeling, scuba diving, and boat tours, or participating in outdoor activities like hiking and biking.

The Amalfi Coast is also home to several cultural and artistic events throughout the year, including concerts, festivals, and art exhibitions. These events offer visitors the chance to experience local culture and traditions and enjoy the region's vibrant arts scene.

Finally, the Amalfi Coast is known for its beautiful natural surroundings. Many visitors enjoy exploring the region's parks and nature reserves, such as the Parco Nazionale del Cilento e Vallo di Diano, which is home to many rare and endangered species.

Overall, there are many activities and attractions for tourists visiting the Amalfi Coast, making it a diverse and exciting destination with something for everyone.

How to Prepare for the Amalfi Coast

Here are a few tips to help you prepare for a visit to the Amalfi Coast:

Pack appropriately:

The weather on the Amalfi Coast can vary, so it is important to pack a range of clothes to cover different weather conditions. Be sure to pack comfortable shoes, as the roads on the Amalfi Coast can be narrow and winding.

Make transportation arrangements:

Consider how you will get around the Amalfi Coast. If you plan to rent a car, be sure to book in advance and make sure you are comfortable driving on narrow and winding roads. If you prefer to use public transportation, be sure to research the bus routes and schedules ahead of time.

Plan your activities:

The Amalfi Coast has a lot to offer, from beautiful beaches to delicious Italian cuisine. Make a list of the activities and attractions that interest you most and plan your itinerary accordingly.

Research accommodation options:

The Amalfi Coast has various accommodation options, from luxury hotels to budget-friendly guesthouses. Research your options and book your accommodation in advance to ensure availability.

Learn a few basic phrases in Italian:

While many locals on the Amalfi Coast speak English, it can be helpful to know a few basic phrases in Italian to get around. Some useful phrases to know include "Buongiorno" (good morning), "Grazie" (thank you), and "Per favore" (please).

Get travel insurance:

It is always a good idea to have travel insurance when traveling abroad in case of any unexpected events or emergencies. Be sure to research your options and choose a policy that meets your needs.

Know your budget:

The Amalfi Coast is a popular tourist destination and can be expensive, especially during peak season. Know your budget and plan your activities and expenses accordingly.

Check the weather:

The weather on the Amalfi Coast can vary depending on the time of year. Check the forecast before you go and pack accordingly.

Respect local customs:

The Amalfi Coast is home to a unique and vibrant culture, and it is essential to respect local customs and traditions when visiting.

Stay safe:

The Amalfi Coast is generally a safe destination, but it is always a good idea to be aware of your surroundings and take basic safety precautions. Avoid walking alone at night, keep your valuables secure, and be mindful of your surroundings when out and about.

By following these tips, you can help ensure that your visit to the Amalfi Coast is well-planned and enjoyable.

Budget Friendly Stays

Here are a few tips for finding budget-friendly accommodations on the Amalfi Coast:

Consider staying in a smaller town:

Positano and Amalfi are some of the most popular cities on the Amalfi Coast, so accommodations can be higher in these areas. Consider staying in a smaller town like Maiori or Minori, where prices may be more reasonable.

Look for deals and discounts:

Many hotels offer discounts for booking in advance or for staying for a longer period of time. Keep an eye out for deals and promotions, and consider booking your stay during the shoulder season (April to May or September to October) when prices are generally lower.

Consider alternative accommodations:

In addition to traditional hotels, there are also many other types of accommodations available on the Amalfi Coast, including bed and breakfasts, vacation rentals, and hostels. These options are often more budget-friendly than traditional hotels.

Use online resources to compare prices:

Several online resources, such as booking websites and comparison sites, can help you find the best prices for accommodations on the Amalfi Coast. Take the time to compare prices and read reviews to find the best deal.

Consider staying in a self-catering apartment:

Renting an apartment with a kitchen allows you to save money by cooking your own meals instead of eating out all the time. This can be a perfect option if you're traveling with a group and can split the rental cost.

Look for hostels:

While hostels may not be as luxurious as traditional hotels, they can be a budget-friendly option for travelers who are willing to share a room or bathroom with other travelers. Many hostels also offer private rooms for a slightly higher price.

Book a package deal:

Many travel companies offer package deals that include flights, accommodation, and other travel services. These packages are often more budget-friendly than booking everything separately.

Consider staying in a nearby city:

If you cannot find budget-friendly accommodations on the Amalfi Coast itself, consider staying in a nearby town and taking day trips to the coast. Cities like Naples, Salerno, and Sorrento are all within easy reach of the Amalfi Coast and may have more budget-friendly accommodation options.

Remember also to consider the location and amenities of the hotel when choosing your accommodations. While finding a budget-friendly option is important, you also want to ensure that you're staying in a safe and convenient location and that the hotel has the amenities you need.

Must see beaches

The Amalfi Coast is known for its beautiful beaches, each with its own character and appeal. Some of the must-visit beaches on the Amalfi Coast include:

Spiaggia Grande: Located in Positano, this is one of the most popular beaches on the Amalfi Coast, known for its soft, golden sands and crystal clear waters. It is also home to many restaurants and beach clubs, making it a great place to relax and enjoy the local food and drink.

Marina di Praia: This beach is located in the town of Praiano, and is known for its stunning views of the coast and crystal clear waters. It is a popular spot for swimming and snorkeling and is also home to many beach clubs and restaurants.

Furore Beach: This beach is located in the town of Furore and is known for its beautiful setting and crystal-clear waters. It is a popular spot for swimming and sunbathing and is also home to several restaurants and cafes.

Duoglio Beach: Located in the town of Maiori, this beach is known for its beautiful setting and clean waters. It is a popular spot for swimming and sunbathing and is also home to several restaurants and cafes.

Conca dei Marini Beach: This small beach is located in the town of Conca dei Marini, and is known for its stunning setting and crystal clear waters. It is a popular spot for swimming and sunbathing, and is also home to several restaurants and cafes.

Santa Croce Beach: This small beach is located in the town of Amalfi and is known for its beautiful setting and crystal-clear waters. It is a popular spot for swimming and sunbathing and is also home to several restaurants and cafes.

Gavitella Beach: This small beach is located in the town of Positano and is known for its beautiful setting and crystal-clear waters. It is a popular spot for swimming and sunbathing and is also home to several restaurants and cafes.

Arienzo Beach: Located in the town of Praiano, this beach is known for its stunning views of the coast and its crystal-clear waters. It is a popular spot for swimming and snorkeling and is also home to several beach clubs and restaurants.

San Francesco Beach: This small beach is located in the town of Amalfi and is known for its beautiful setting and crystal-clear waters. It is a popular spot for swimming and sunbathing and is also home to several restaurants and cafes.

Minori Beach: Located in the town of Minori, this beach is known for its beautiful setting and crystal-clear waters. It is a popular spot for swimming and sunbathing and is also home to several restaurants and cafes.

Overall, the Amalfi Coast is home to many beautiful beaches, each with its own unique charm and appeal. There is something for everyone, whether you are looking for a secluded cove, a sandy beach, or a bustling beach club.

Must See Beaches

The Amalfi Coast is known for its beautiful beaches, each with its own character and appeal. Some of the must-visit beaches on the Amalfi Coast include:

Spiaggia Grande:

Located in Positano, this is one of the most popular beaches on the Amalfi Coast, known for its soft, golden sands and crystal clear waters. It is also home to many restaurants and beach clubs, making it a great place to relax and enjoy the local food and drink.

Marina di Praia:

This beach is located in the town of Praiano and is known for its stunning views of the coast and crystal clear waters. It is a popular spot for swimming and snorkeling and is also home to many beach clubs and restaurants.

Furore Beach:

This beach is located in the town of Furore and is known for its beautiful setting and crystal-clear waters. It is a popular spot for swimming and sunbathing and is also home to several restaurants and cafes.

Duoglio Beach:

Located in the town of Maiori, this beach is known for its beautiful setting and clean waters. It is a popular spot for swimming and sunbathing and is also home to several restaurants and cafes.

Conca dei Marini Beach:

This small beach is located in the town of Conca dei Marini and is known for its stunning setting and crystal-clear waters. It is a popular spot for swimming and sunbathing and is also home to several restaurants and cafes.

Santa Croce Beach:

This small beach is located in the town of Amalfi and is known for its beautiful setting and crystal-clear waters. It is a popular spot for swimming and sunbathing and is also home to several restaurants and cafes.

Gavitella Beach:

This small beach is located in the town of Positano and is known for its beautiful setting and crystal-clear waters. It is a popular spot for swimming and sunbathing and is also home to several restaurants and cafes.

Arienzo Beach:

Located in the town of Praiano, this beach is known for its stunning views of the coast and its crystal-clear waters. It is a popular spot for swimming and snorkeling and is also home to several beach clubs and restaurants.

San Francesco Beach:

This small beach is located in the town of Amalfi and is known for its beautiful setting and crystal-clear waters. It is a popular spot for swimming and sunbathing and is also home to several restaurants and cafes.

Minori Beach:

Located in the town of Minori, this beach is known for its beautiful setting and crystal-clear waters. It is a popular spot for swimming and sunbathing and is also home to several restaurants and cafes.

Overall, the Amalfi Coast is home to many beautiful beaches, each with its own unique charm and appeal. There is something for everyone, whether you are looking for a secluded cove, a sandy beach, or a bustling beach club.

Top Restaurants to Visit

The Amalfi Coast is known for its excellent food and wine, with many local restaurants offering delicious local specialties and internationally-renowned wines. Here are the ten top restaurants to visit on the Amalfi Coast:

Da Adolfo:

Da Adolfo is a popular restaurant located in the town of Positano on the Amalfi Coast in Italy. It is known for its delicious seafood dishes and stunning views of the coast.

According to the restaurant's website, Da Adolfo has been in operation since the 1950s and has a long history of serving delicious seafood to its customers. The restaurant is located on a small beach in Positano and is known for its relaxed and casual atmosphere.

In addition to its delicious food, Da Adolfo is also known for its beautiful setting and stunning views of the coast. The restaurant is located on the beach and has outdoor seating that offers panoramic sea views.

Overall, Da Adolfo is a popular and well-respected restaurant on the Amalfi Coast, known for its delicious seafood dishes and beautiful setting.

Ristorante Eolo:

Ristorante Eolo is a popular restaurant located in the town of Amalfi on the Amalfi Coast in Italy. It is known for its delicious Italian dishes and excellent wines.

According to the restaurant's website, Ristorante Eolo was founded in the 1970s by the Capobianco family, who have a long history of cooking and hospitality on the Amalfi Coast. The restaurant is located in a beautiful building with a terrace that offers panoramic views of the coast.

In addition to its delicious food, Ristorante Eolo is also known for its excellent wine selection, with a wide range of local and international wines available. The restaurant is popular with both tourists and locals and has a reputation for offering high-quality dining and excellent service.

Overall, Ristorante Eolo is a popular and well-respected restaurant on the Amalfi Coast, known for its delicious Italian dishes and excellent wines.

Ristorante Pizzeria Tasso:

Ristorante Pizzeria Tasso is a popular restaurant located in the town of Sorrento on the Amalfi Coast in Italy. It is known for its delicious pizzas and other Italian dishes.

According to the restaurant's website, Ristorante Pizzeria Tasso has been in operation for over 50 years and has a long history of serving delicious pizzas and other Italian dishes to its customers. The restaurant is located in the heart of Sorrento and has a warm and inviting atmosphere.

In addition to its delicious food, Ristorante Pizzeria Tasso is also known for its excellent service and friendly staff. The restaurant is popular with both tourists and locals and has a reputation for offering high-quality dining at reasonable prices.

Overall, Ristorante Pizzeria Tasso is a popular and well-respected restaurant on the Amalfi Coast, known for its delicious pizzas and other Italian dishes.

Ristorante La Conca del Sogno:

Ristorante La Conca del Sogno is a popular restaurant located in the town of Conca dei Marini on the Amalfi Coast in Italy. It is known for its delicious seafood dishes and stunning views of the coast.

According to the restaurant's website, Ristorante La Conca del Sogno has been in operation for over 30 years and has a long history of serving delicious seafood to its customers. The restaurant is located in a beautiful setting with a terrace that offers panoramic views of the coast.

In addition to its delicious food, Ristorante La Conca del Sogno is also known for its excellent service and friendly staff. The restaurant is popular with both tourists and locals and has a reputation for offering high-quality dining and a beautiful setting.

Overall, Ristorante La Conca del Sogno is a popular and well-respected restaurant on the Amalfi Coast, known for its delicious seafood dishes and stunning views of the coast.

Ristorante La Sponda:

Ristorante La Sponda is a popular restaurant located in the town of Positano on the Amalfi Coast in Italy. It is known for its delicious Italian dishes and excellent wines.

According to the restaurant's website, Ristorante La Sponda has a long history of serving high-quality Italian cuisine to its customers. The restaurant is located in a beautiful setting with a terrace that offers panoramic views of the coast.

In addition to its delicious food, Ristorante La Sponda is also known for its excellent wine selection, with a wide range of local and international wines available. The restaurant is popular with tourists and locals alike and has a reputation for offering high-quality dining and excellent service.

Overall, Ristorante La Sponda is a popular and well-respected restaurant on the Amalfi Coast, known for its delicious Italian dishes and excellent wines.

Ristorante Il Ritrovo:

Ristorante Il Ritrovo is a popular restaurant located in the town of Ravello on the Amalfi Coast in Italy. It is known for its delicious Italian dishes and excellent wines.

According to the restaurant's website, Ristorante Il Ritrovo has a long history of serving high-quality Italian cuisine to its customers. The restaurant is located in a beautiful setting with a terrace that offers panoramic views of the coast.

In addition to its delicious food, Ristorante Il Ritrovo is also known for its excellent wine selection, with a wide range of local and international wines available. The restaurant is popular with tourists and locals alike and has a reputation for offering high-quality dining and excellent service.

Overall, Ristorante Il Ritrovo is a popular and well-respected restaurant on the Amalfi Coast, known for its delicious Italian dishes and excellent wines.

Ristorante Don Alfonso 1890:

Ristorante Don Alfonso 1890 is a popular restaurant located in the town of Sant'Agata sui Due Golfi on the Amalfi Coast in Italy. It is known for its delicious Italian dishes and excellent wines.

According to the restaurant's website, Ristorante Don Alfonso 1890 was founded in 1890 by the Iaccarino family, who have a long history of cooking and hospitality on the Amalfi Coast. The restaurant is located in a beautiful setting with a terrace that offers panoramic views of the coast.

In addition to its delicious food, Ristorante Don Alfonso 1890 is also known for its excellent wine selection, with a wide range of local and international wines available. The restaurant is popular with tourists and locals alike and has a reputation for offering high-quality dining and excellent service.

Overall, Ristorante Don Alfonso 1890 is a popular and well-respected restaurant on the Amalfi Coast, known for its delicious Italian dishes and excellent wines.

Ristorante La Caravella:

Ristorante La Caravella is a popular restaurant located in the town of Amalfi on the Amalfi Coast in Italy. It is known for its delicious seafood dishes and excellent wines.

According to the restaurant's website, Ristorante La Caravella has been in operation for over 50 years and has a long history of serving delicious seafood to its customers. The restaurant is located in a beautiful setting with a terrace that offers panoramic views of the coast.

In addition to its delicious food, Ristorante La Caravella is also known for its excellent wine selection, with a wide range of local and international wines available. The restaurant is popular with tourists and locals alike and has a reputation for offering high-quality dining and excellent service.

Overall, Ristorante La Caravella is a popular and well-respected restaurant on the Amalfi Coast, known for its delicious seafood dishes and excellent wines.

Ristorante Pizzeria Da Maria:

Ristorante Pizzeria Da Maria is a popular restaurant located in the town of Praiano on the Amalfi Coast in Italy. It is known for its delicious pizzas and other Italian dishes.

According to the restaurant's website, Ristorante Pizzeria Da Maria has been in operation for over 30 years and has a long history of serving delicious pizzas and other Italian dishes to its customers. The restaurant is located in a beautiful setting with a terrace that offers panoramic views of the coast.

In addition to its delicious food, Ristorante Pizzeria Da Maria is also known for its excellent service and friendly staff. The restaurant is popular with both tourists and locals and has a reputation for offering high-quality dining at reasonable prices.

Overall, Ristorante Pizzeria Da Maria is a popular and well-respected restaurant on the Amalfi Coast, known for its delicious pizzas and other Italian dishes.

Ristorante Da Vincenzo:

Ristorante Da Vincenzo is a popular restaurant located in the town of Sorrento on the Amalfi Coast in Italy. It is known for its delicious Italian dishes and excellent wines.

According to the restaurant's website, Ristorante Da Vincenzo has a long history of serving high-quality Italian cuisine to its customers. The restaurant is located in a beautiful setting with a terrace that offers panoramic views of the coast.

In addition to its delicious food, Ristorante Da Vincenzo is also known for its excellent wine selection, with a wide range of local and international wines available. The restaurant is popular with tourists and locals alike and has a reputation for offering high-quality dining and excellent service.

Overall, Ristorante Da Vincenzo is a popular and well-respected restaurant on the Amalfi Coast, known for its delicious Italian dishes and excellent wines.

These are just a few excellent restaurants visitors can enjoy on the Amalfi Coast. The region is known for its delicious food and excellent wines, making it a must-visit destination for foodies.

What to Avoid When on Your Travels

There are a few things that tourists visiting the Amalfi Coast should be aware of and try to avoid in order to have a safe and enjoyable trip. Here are a few suggestions:

Avoid overloading on souvenirs:

While it can be tempting to buy souvenirs for yourself and your loved ones, be mindful of the weight of your luggage and try to avoid overloading with souvenirs, especially if you have a lot of travel planned.

Avoid walking in the middle of the road:

The roads on the Amalfi Coast can be narrow and winding, and it is essential to be aware of your surroundings when walking. Try to avoid walking in the middle of the road and stay on the sidewalk whenever possible.

Avoid leaving valuables in plain sight:

While the Amalfi Coast is generally a safe destination, it is always a good idea to be cautious and avoid leaving valuables in plain sight when out and about. Keep your wallet, passport, and other valuables in a secure place when not in use.

Avoid getting too close to the edge of cliffs:

The Amalfi Coast is home to many beautiful and scenic cliffs, but it is important to be mindful of your surroundings and avoid getting too close to the edge.

Avoid overspending:

It can be easy to get carried away when on vacation, but be mindful of your budget and try to avoid overspending on unnecessary items.

Avoid visiting during the peak tourist season:

The Amalfi Coast is popular with tourists and can get very crowded during the peak tourist season. If you want to avoid the crowds, consider visiting outside of the peak season, when the weather is still pleasant, and the crowds are smaller.

Avoid wearing high heels:

The roads on the Amalfi Coast can be narrow and winding, and the pavements can be uneven. Wearing high heels can make it challenging to navigate the streets and can be dangerous, so it is best to avoid them.

Avoid overdoing it on the sun:

The Amalfi Coast is known for its sunny weather, but it is important to be mindful of your skin and avoid overdoing it in the sun. Wear sunscreen, wear a hat, and try to stay in the shade during the hottest parts of the day.

Avoid trying to drive if you are not comfortable:

The roads on the Amalfi Coast can be narrow and winding, and driving can be challenging if you are uncomfortable behind the wheel. If you need more confidence driving on these roads, consider using public transportation or hiring a driver.

Avoid being too rigid with your travel plans:

While it is always a good idea to have a rough plan when traveling, try to be flexible and avoid being too strict with your travel plans. This will allow you to be open to new experiences and make the most of your trip.

By following these simple tips, tourists visiting the Amalfi Coast can help ensure a safe and enjoyable.

The Best Way to Travel When Visiting the Amalfi Coast

There are a few different ways to travel on the Amalfi Coast, and the best option for you will depend on your personal preferences and budget. Here are a few options to consider:

Bus:

The Amalfi Coast is served by several bus routes, which can be a convenient and economical way to get around the region. The buses run frequently and can take you to many of the major towns and villages on the coast.

Car:

If you are comfortable driving on winding and narrow roads, renting a car can be an excellent way to explore the Amalfi Coast. This gives you more freedom and flexibility to visit the destinations that interest you most.

Boat:

The Amalfi Coast is home to many small ports, and it is possible to travel between the towns and villages by boat. This can be a fun and scenic way to explore the coast and offers the opportunity to see the region from a different perspective.

Private tour:

If you want a more organized and guided experience, consider booking a private tour of the Amalfi Coast. This can be a good option if you are not comfortable navigating the region on your own or if you want to learn more about the history and culture of the area.

The best way to travel on the Amalfi Coast will depend on your personal preferences and budget. Consider your options and choose the method that best suits your needs.

Fun Facts About The Amalfi Coast

Here are a few fun facts about the Amalfi Coast:

1. The Amalfi Coast was designated as a UNESCO World Heritage Site in 1997 due to its unique and beautiful landscape, which includes a mix of cliffs, beaches, and small villages.

2. The Amalfi Coast is home to many lemon groves producing the famous Sorrento lemons. These lemons are used to make various products, including lemon liqueur and lemon-scented cleaning products.

3. The Amalfi Coast is known for its beautiful beaches, including the beach at Positano, which is often called one of the most beautiful beaches in the world.

4. The Amalfi Coast is home to many small villages, each

with its own unique character and history. The village of Ravello is known for its beautiful gardens and stunning views, while the village of Amalfi is known for its beautiful cathedral and bustling streets.

5. The Amalfi Coast is a popular destination for celebrities, with many famous actors, musicians, and other celebrities choosing to vacation there.

6. The Amalfi Coast is home to many excellent restaurants that specialize in seafood dishes. The region is also known for its superb wines, including the famous limoncello liqueur.

7. The Amalfi Coast is known for its beautiful sunsets, with many tourists visiting the region to experience the stunning views at sunset.

8. The Amalfi Coast is home to many beautiful and historic churches, including the Church of Santa Maria Assunta in Positano and the Duomo di Amalfi in Amalfi.

9. The Amalfi Coast is known for its beautiful and fragrant flowers, including the bougainvillea and the oleander. These flowers can be found throughout the region and add to the region's colorful and vibrant atmosphere.

10.

The Amalfi Coast is home to many beautiful and scenic hiking trails, including the Path of the Gods, which offers stunning views of the coast.

11. The Amalfi Coast is known for its beautiful and colorful houses, which are often painted in bright shades of pink, yellow, and blue.

12. The Amalfi Coast is home to many beautiful and historic villas, many of which have been converted into luxury hotels. These villas offer stunning views of the coast and are a popular choice for tourists looking for a luxurious and relaxing vacation.

13. The Amalfi Coast is known for its beautiful clear waters, perfect for swimming, snorkeling, and other water sports.

14. The Amalfi Coast is home to many beautiful and scenic drives, including the winding road that connects the towns of Posit.

What the locals love about the tourists

The locals on the Amalfi Coast likely appreciate the economic benefits that tourists bring to the region, as tourism is an important industry on the Amalfi Coast. Tourists support local businesses, such as restaurants, hotels, and souvenir shops, which provide employment and income for the locals.

Tourists also bring excitement and diversity to the region, introducing locals to new cultures and ways of life. Many locals may enjoy interacting with tourists and learning about their experiences and backgrounds.

Additionally, tourists bring new ideas and perspectives to the region, stimulating cultural exchange and fostering a sense of community.

Overall, it is likely that the locals on the Amalfi Coast appreciate the economic and cultural benefits that tourists bring to the region.

Conclusion

In conclusion, the Amalfi Coast is a beautiful and vibrant southern Italy region known for its stunning landscape, delicious Italian cuisine, and excellent wines. The region is home to several small villages and towns, each with its own unique character and history. It is a popular tourist destination known for its beautiful beaches, beautiful sunsets, and clear waters.

There are several different ways to travel on the Amalfi Coast, including by bus, car, boat, or private tour. The region is also home to many excellent restaurants and luxurious hotels, offering visitors a range of options for dining and accommodation.

Whether you are looking for a relaxing beach vacation, a culinary adventure, or a chance to immerse yourself in the history and culture of the region, the Amalfi Coast has something to offer. With its beautiful landscapes, delicious food, and rich history, the Amalfi Coast is a must-visit destination for anyone looking to explore all Italy has to offer.

Review

Thank you for reading this pocket travel guide to the Amalfi Coast. We hope that you have found it helpful and informative and has inspired you to visit this beautiful and vibrant region.

If you have enjoyed reading this travel guide and it has provided you with value, we would appreciate it if you could leave a review. Your feedback helps us improve our travel guides and ensures that we provide valuable and accurate information to our readers. It also helps others receive the best guide when on their travels.

Scroll down on the books page and click on the "Leave a Review" button to leave a review. Your feedback is greatly appreciated, and we look forward to helping you plan your next trip to the Amalfi Coast.

References

Basic Italian Words and Phrases for Your Trip to Italy. (2020, October 1). Travel + Leisure.

Cruises, C. (2022, August 15). 15 Best Beaches on the Amalfi Coast. Celebrity Current.

Grant, L. (2019, October 3). 8 Rookie Mistakes to Avoid in the Amalfi Coast. Oyster.com.

Gray, M. (2017, May 17). Must-Visit Restaurants on the Amalfi Coast. Culture Trip.

Shaw, B. (2022, November 9). The 20 Best Restaurants on the Amalfi Coast. The Tour Guy.

Smith, H. (2022, August 15). 16 tips for planning your trip to the Amalfi Coast. Lonely Planet. https://www.lonelyplanet.com/art icles/planning-perfect-trip-amalfi-coast-italy

Made in the USA
Monee, IL
07 April 2023

31514045R00038